NFL Teams

WASHINGTON FOOTBALL TEAM

KENNY ABDO

Fly!
An Imprint of Abdo Zoom
abdobooks.com

abdobooks.com

Published by Abdo Zoom, a division of ABDO, P.O. Box 398166, Minneapolis, Minnesota 55439. Copyright © 2022 by Abdo Consulting Group, Inc. International copyrights reserved in all countries. No part of this book may be reproduced in any form without written permission from the publisher. Fly!™ is a trademark and logo of Abdo Zoom.

Printed in the United States of America, North Mankato, Minnesota.
052021
092021

Photo Credits: AP Images, Getty Images, Icon Sportswire, iStock, Shutterstock PREMIER
Production Contributors: Kenny Abdo, Jennie Forsberg, Grace Hansen
Design Contributors: Candice Keimig, Neil Klinepier

Library of Congress Control Number: 2020919723t

Publisher's Cataloging-in-Publication Data

Names: Abdo, Kenny, author.
Title: Washington Football Team / by Kenny Abdo.
Description: Minneapolis, Minnesota : Abdo Zoom, 2022 | Series: NFL teams | Includes online resources and index.
Identifiers: ISBN 9781098224820 (lib. bdg.) | ISBN 9781098225766 (ebook) | ISBN 9781098226237 (Read-to-Me ebook)
Subjects: LCSH: National Football League--Juvenile literature. | Football teams--Juvenile literature. | American football--Juvenile literature. | Professional sports-Juvenile literature.
Classification: DDC 796.33264--dc23

TABLE OF CONTENTS

Washington Football Team 4

Kick Off.......................... 8

Team Recaps 14

Hall of Fame 24

Glossary 30

Online Resources 31

Index 32

WASHINGTON FOOTBALL TEAM

For more than 90 years, the Washington Football Team has excited fans with iconic players, historic records, and thrilling victories!

As one of the sport's oldest teams, Washington has won two NFL **Championships** and three **Super Bowls** for the nation's capital!

KICK OFF

The team was founded in 1932 by George Preston Marshall. Known as the Boston Braves, the team was first based in Massachusetts.

In 1937, Marshall moved the team to Washington DC. The team did well in its new home. In the season opener, Washington beat the New York Giants 13-3.

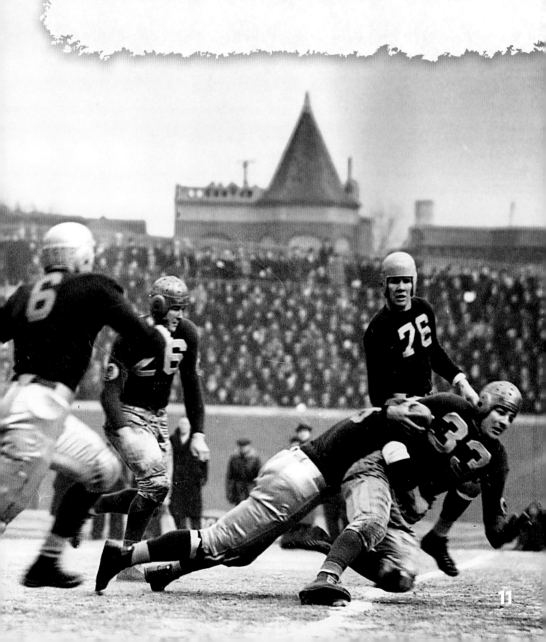

With a newly-**drafted** star **quarterback**, Sammy Baugh, the season just kept getting better. Washington went on to win the **championship** that first season in DC. In 1942, Baugh led the team to a second championship win!

TEAM RECAPS

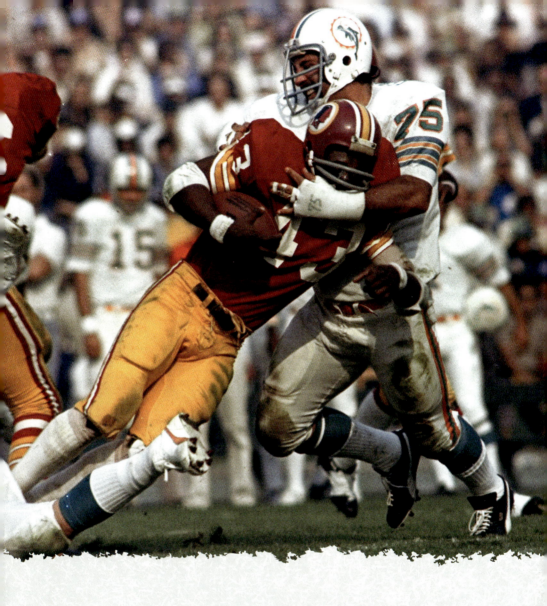

Washington lost the **Championship** games in 1943 and 1945. They wouldn't see a championship or playoff game for another 25 years. Following the 1972 season, they went to the **Super Bowl**! Sadly, they lost to the Dolphins.

Washington made a second Big Game appearance at **Super Bowl** XVII. They played against the Dolphins again and this time Washington won 27-17!

Following the 1987 season, Washington made it to **Super Bowl** XXII and beat the Broncos 42-10. Four years later, Washington was back at the Super Bowl. They beat the Bills earning an incredible third NFL title in 10 seasons!

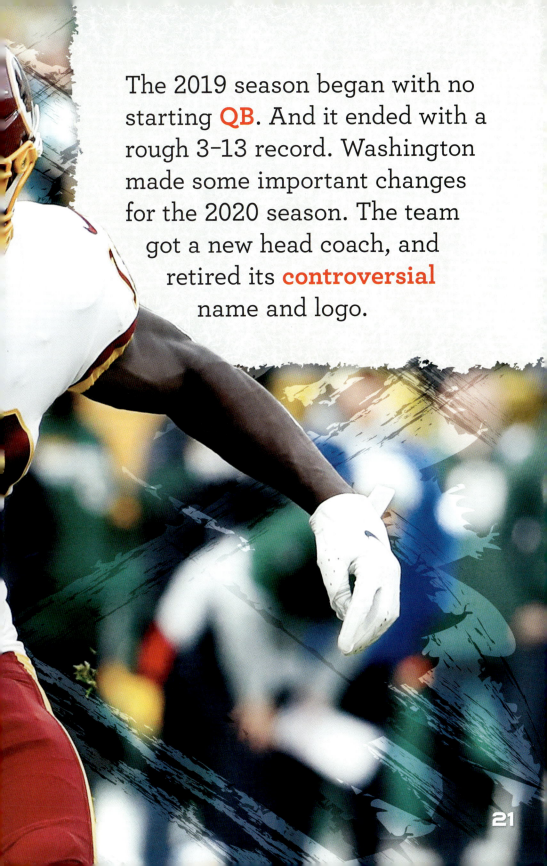

The 2019 season began with no starting **QB**. And it ended with a rough 3-13 record. Washington made some important changes for the 2020 season. The team got a new head coach, and retired its **controversial** name and logo.

Washington ended the 2020 season first in the **NFC** East division. With a new name, look, and **QB** on the horizon, the future looks bright for the long running team!

HALL OF FAME

QB Joe Theismann played for Washington his entire NFL career. He led the team to two **Super Bowls** and helped win one. By the time he retired, he had thrown for 25,206 yards, more than any other Washington QB.

Wide receiver Art Monk had 58 receptions his first season, a record for a Washington **rookie**. Monk helped Washington win three **Super Bowls**. For years, he held NFL records for most catches in a season and most catches in a career. Monk was **inducted** into the Pro Football Hall of Fame in 2008.

Cornerback Darrell Green caught an **interception** in 19 of his 20 seasons with Washington, with 54 interceptions in all. That is more than any Washington player. Green helped the team make it to three **Super Bowls**, winning two. Green was **inducted** into the Pro Football Hall of Fame in 2008.

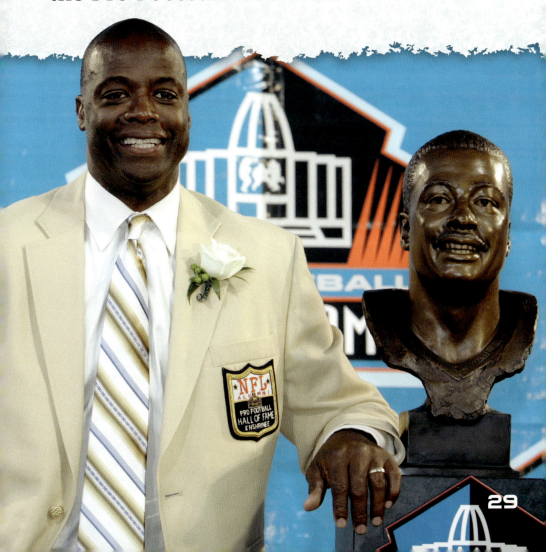

GLOSSARY

championship – a game held to find a first-place winner.

controversial – relating to controversy, which is a discussion marked by disagreement and debate.

draft – a process in sports to assign athletes to a certain team.

induct – to admit someone as a member of an organization.

interception – when a player catches a pass that was meant for the other team's player.

National Football Conference (NFC) – one of two major conferences of the NFL. Each conference contains 16 teams split into four divisions. The winner of the NFC championship plays the AFC winner at the Super Bowl.

quarterback (QB) – the player on the offensive team that directs teammates in their play.

rookie – a first-year player in a professional sport.

Super Bowl – the NFL championship game, played once a year.

ONLINE RESOURCES

To learn more about the Washington Football Team, please visit **abdobooklinks.com** or scan this QR code. These links are routinely monitored and updated to provide the most current information available.

INDEX

Baugh, Sammy 13

Bills (team) 19

Broncos (team) 19

Dolphins (team) 15, 17

Green, Darrell 29

Marshall, George Preston 8, 11

Monk, Art 26

Super Bowl 7, 15, 17, 19, 25, 26, 29

Theismann, Joe 25